A REVIEW OF THE COVID-19 VACCINE MANDATES IN THE FRAMEWORK OF THE RIGHT TO BODILY AUTONOMY

VOLUME 2, ISSUE 4 OF BRILLOPEDIA

NAYAB NASEER

Contents

Preface

"Start writing, no matter what. The water does not flow until the faucet is turned on".

• Louis L'Amour

Hundreds of students and professors are contributing their work to Brillopedia, we are here to provide ample information about Law and Contemporary issues. Our aim is to provide a platform for today's generation to express their views and ideas on law and contemporary law.

CHAPTER ONE

Abstract

The right to bodily autonomy is the right for individuals to make decisions about their own bodies and medical treatment, including the right to refuse or consent to such treatment. This right is recognized in national laws and international human rights instruments, and is closely related to the right to privacy. Most constitutions and legal frameworks worldwide accept the right to bodily autonomy as a fundamental right. The right, based on the principle of informed consent, closely relates to the right to privacy and holds than an individual has the right to make decisions on their own bodies, including the right to consent or refuse to any medical procedures or treatment. International conventions such as the International Covenant on Civil and Political Rights, Convention on the Rights of the Child, and the European Convention on Human Rights affirm the right to bodily autonomy.

In the United Kingdom, the principle of autonomy is recognized in common law and is reflected in statues such as the Human Rights Act 1998 and the Mental Capacity Act 2005. In the United States, the right to bodily autonomy is protected by the Due Process Clause of the Fourteenth Amendment to the U.S. Constitution, which guarantees the right to liberty and prohibits the government from depriving individuals of life, liberty, or property without due process of law.

In India, the right to bodily autonomy is protected by the Constitution of India through fundamental rights, including the right to life, personal liberty, and privacy. Landmark judgments on the right to bodily autonomy from courts around the world have helped to establish and protect this fundamental human right.

COVID-19 vaccine mandates that require individuals to be vaccinated against the coronavirus disease (COVID-19) have been the subject of legal challenges in many cases. These challenges argue that vaccine mandates violate the right to bodily autonomy or other legal rights. The question of the balance between the right to privacy and bodily autonomy and the responsibility of governments to protect public health has been central to these challenges.

The U.K. did not introduce COVID vaccine mandates. In the United States, the Occupational Safety and Health Authority (OSHA) had imposed a mandate requiring that workers at businesses with 100 or more employees get vaccinated or submit a negative COVID test weekly to enter the workplace. The U.S. Supreme Court, in the National Federation of Business vs the Department of Labor, blocked this mandate.

In India, the Supreme Court upheld the right to bodily autonomy and ruled that the government cannot make COVID vaccination mandatory. The Court stated that the government can only provide information about the benefits of vaccination and persuade individuals to get vaccinated but cannot force them to do so.

CHAPTER TWO

What is the right to bodily autonomy?

The right to bodily autonomy, also known as the right to self-determination or the right to control one's body, is a fundamental human right recognised in several national laws and international human rights instruments[1].

In general, laws protecting the right to bodily autonomy recognise that individuals have the right to make decisions about their own bodies, including medical treatment and other personal matters. This includes the right to refuse medical treatment or procedures, as well as the right to consent to them.

The right to bodily autonomy is closely related to the right to privacy, which is concerned with protecting personal information and being left alone. The right to privacy includes the right to control the dissemination of personal information and freedom from surveillance and interference in one's personal life.

[1] Dr. Natalia Kanem, Bodily autonomy: A fundamental right, United Nations Population Fund (Dec 28, 2022, 19:43), https://www.unfpa.org/press/bodily-autonomy-fundamental-right

CHAPTER THREE

Principle of informed consent

The "grundnorm" for the right to bodily autonomy is the principle of informed consent and non-malfeasance[1]. This requires healthcare professionals to respect their patient's autonomy and ensure that they are fully informed about their treatment options and the risks and benefits of each option. These principles reflect in codes of ethics and professional standards for healthcare professionals, which set out the obligations of healthcare professionals to respect their patients' autonomy.

Legal framework on the right to bodily autonomy

The right to bodily autonomy is recognised as a fundamental human right and gets protection through international human rights laws, conventions, and positive laws enacted by nation-states.

CHAPTER FOUR

International conventions

The international human rights laws and conventions that protect the right to bodily autonomy are:

1. International Covenant on Civil and Political Rights (ICCPR)[1]: This treaty, which is binding on states that have ratified it, recognises the right to self-determination and the right to be free from torture or cruel, inhuman or degrading treatment or punishment. These rights are relevant to protecting bodily autonomy, as they allow individuals to make their own decisions about their bodies and medical treatment and prohibit the state from inflicting harm on individuals.

2. Convention on the Rights of the Child (CRC)[2]: This treaty, which is binding on states that have ratified it, recognizes children's right to protection from all forms of physical or mental violence, injury or abuse. The CRC also recognizes children's right to the highest attainable health standard and enjoyment of the highest possible physical and mental health standard. These rights are relevant to the protection of the bodily autonomy of children, as they ensure that children have the right to make their own decisions about their healthcare and remain protected from harm.

National laws

Most countries worldwide have national laws that provide for the protection of the right to bodily autonomy. These laws may include provisions that recognise the right to refuse medical treatment, consent to medical treatment, and access healthcare services.

CHAPTER FIVE

Position in the United Kingdom

The primary legal protection for the right to bodily autonomy in the U.K. is the principle of autonomy, recognized in the common law. This principle holds that individuals have the right to make their own decisions about their bodies and medical treatment and to have those decisions respected by others.

The Human Rights Act 1998[1] protects the right to bodily autonomy by incorporating the European Convention on Human Rights into U.K. law. The Convention includes several provisions relating to the right to respect for private and family life, including the right to respect for physical and moral integrity (Article 8).

The principle of autonomy also reflects in the Mental Capacity Act 2005[2], which applies to adults who lack the capacity to make decisions about their care and treatment. The Act provides a framework for decision-making on behalf of individuals unable to make decisions for them and requires that any decisions made on their behalf must be in their best interests and consider their past and present wishes, feelings, values, and beliefs.

[1] The Human Rights Act, 1988, Acts of Parliament, 1988, United Kingdom.

[2] Mental Capability Act, 2005, Acts of Parliament, 2005, United Kingdom.

CHAPTER SIX

Position in the United States

The U.S. Constitution protects the right to bodily autonomy through the Due Process Clause of the Fourteenth Amendment[1], which guarantees the right to liberty and prohibits the government from depriving individuals of life, liberty, or property without due process of law. The courts interpreted this protection to include the right to be free from unwanted medical treatment or procedures.

The principle of informed consent is reflected in various federal and state laws and regulations and in ethical guidelines for healthcare professionals.

CHAPTER SEVEN

Position in India

The Constitution of India protects the right to bodily autonomy through fundamental rights. Article 21 establishes the right to life, personal liberty, and privacy. The courts have interpreted these protections to include the right to be free from unwanted medical treatment or procedures.

<u>Judicial verdicts on the right to bodily autonomy</u>

Several landmark judgments on the right to bodily autonomy from courts around the world have helped to establish and protect this fundamental human right.

<u>Landmark judgments on bodily autonomy from the Supreme Court of India</u>

There have been several landmark judgments on the right to bodily autonomy in India, which have helped to establish and protect this fundamental human right. Some of the key judgments on the right to bodily autonomy in India are:

1. Gian Kaur v. State of Punjab (1996)[1]: In this case, the Supreme Court of India recognised that the right to bodily autonomy is an inherent part of the right to life and personal liberty protected under Article 21 of the Constitution. The Court held that the state cannot force medical treatment on individuals against their will unless it is necessary to protect their life or health.

2. Aruna Shanbaug v. Union of India (2011)[2]: In this case, the Supreme Court of India recognised that the right to bodily autonomy includes the right to refuse medical treatment, even in cases where the individual is unable to consent to or refuse treatment. The Court held that the state cannot force medical treatment on individuals who are vegetative or unable to express their wishes unless it is necessary to protect their life or health.

3. Supreme Court Women Lawyers Association v. Union of India (2016)[3]: The Supreme Court of India recognised that the right to bodily autonomy includes the right to access abortion services. The Court held that the state has a positive obligation to ensure that individuals have access to safe and legal abortion services and that the state cannot impose undue burdens on individuals seeking to access such services.

4. Navtej Singh Johar v. Union of India (2018)[4]: In this landmark case, the Supreme Court of India recognised that the right to bodily autonomy includes the right to make decisions about one's sexual orientation and gender identity. The Court struck down a colonial-era law that criminalised homosexuality, holding that the law violated individuals' right to privacy and dignity.

Landmark judgments from other parts of the world

Some of the key judgments on the right to bodily autonomy from different countries are:

1. R v. Brown (1993) [5] - United Kingdom: The House of Lords recognised that the right to bodily autonomy includes the right to refuse medical treatment. The Court ruled that individuals have the right to make their own decisions about their medical treatment. The state cannot force medical treatment on individuals against their will unless it is necessary to protect their life or health.

2. 2. A, B and C v. Ireland (2010)[6] - Ireland: In this case, the European Court of Human Rights (ECHR) held that the right to bodily autonomy includes the right to access abortion services in cases where the pregnancy poses a risk to the life or health of the woman. The Court ruled that the state has a positive obligation to ensure that individuals have access to safe and legal abortion services and that the state cannot impose an undue burden on individuals seeking to access such services.

3. R (on the application of Nicklinson and another) v. Ministry of Justice (2014)[7] - United Kingdom: In this case, the Supreme Court of the United Kingdom recognised that the right to bodily autonomy includes the right to refuse medical treatment, even in cases where the individual

is unable to consent to or refuse treatment. The Court held that the state cannot force medical treatment on individuals who are unable to express their wishes unless it is necessary to protect their life or health.

4. Obergefell v. Hodges (2015)[8] - United States: In this landmark case, the Supreme Court of the United States recognised that the right to bodily autonomy includes the right to marry and to have one's marriage recognised by the state. The Court ruled that same-sex couples have the same right to marry as opposite-sex couples and that the state cannot deny marriage licenses to same-sex couples based on their sexual orientation.

[1] Gian Kaur v. State of Punjab, (1996) 2 SCC 648

[2] Aruna Shanbaug v. Union of India, (2011) 4 SCC 454.

[3] Supreme Court Women Lawyers Association v. Union of India, (2016) 5 SCC 479.

[4] Navtej Singh Johar v. Union of India, (2018) 10 SCC 1.

[5] Regina v Brown [1993] UKHL 19

[6] A, B and C v. Ireland, (2010) ECHR 2065.

[7] R (on the application of Nicklinson and another) v. Ministry of Justice [2014] EWCA Civ 961

[8] Obergefell v. Hodges, 576 U.S. ___ (2015)

CHAPTER EIGHT

The COVID-19 vaccine mandates as a flashpoint in the right to bodily autonomy and privacy

COVID-19, also known as coronavirus, is a highly infectious respiratory illness caused by the severe acute respiratory syndrome coronavirus 2 (SARS-CoV-2). It was first identified in Wuhan, China, in 2019 and has since become a global pandemic, affecting millions worldwide[1].

COVID-19 vaccine mandates refer to laws, regulations, or policies that require individuals to be vaccinated against the coronavirus disease (COVID-19) in certain circumstances. These mandates can vary in scope and apply to specific groups, such as healthcare workers, schoolchildren, or the general population[2].

Many countries and states implemented COVID-19 vaccine mandates to help control the spread of the virus and protect public health. These mandates can take various forms, such as requiring individuals to be vaccinated to attend school or work in specific settings or requiring proof of vaccination for certain activities or events.

COVID-19 vaccine mandates have been the subject of legal challenges in some cases, with some individuals or groups arguing that they violate the right to bodily autonomy or other legal rights. The critical question confronting the judges was the balance between the right to privacy and bodily autonomy and the responsibility of governments to protect public health.

On the one hand, the right to privacy is an important aspect of personal freedom and bodily autonomy. Individuals have the right to make their own decisions about their health and medical treatment.

Governments across the world introduced vaccine mandates to protect public health and ensure the well-being of their citizens. In many cases, authorities implemented vaccine mandates to achieve herd immunity and control the spread of the virus. Some governments have implemented vaccine mandates for certain occupations or activities, such as healthcare workers or international travel, to protect vulnerable populations or prevent the spread of the virus.

Many individuals and rights activists challenged the legality of vaccine mandates in courts worldwide.

[1] World Health Organization, https://www.who.int/news-room/questions-and-answers/item/coronavirus-disease-covid-19-how-is-it-transmitted (Last visited Dec 28, 2022).

[2] WebMD, https://www.webmd.com/vaccines/covid-19-vaccine/vaccine-mandates (last visited Dec 28, 2022).

CHAPTER NINE

U.S. Supreme Court verdicts on vaccine mandates

In the USA, the Occupational Safety and Health Authority (OSHA) had imposed a mandate requiring that workers at businesses with 100 or more employees get vaccinated or submit a negative COVID test weekly to enter the workplace. The Supreme Court, in *the National Federation of Business vs the Department of Labor*[1], blocked the sweeping vaccine-or-test requirements, effectively doing away with vaccine mandates in the private sector. The majority of the judges in the 6-3 split verdict opined that the U.S. Congress only intended to give OSHA the power to address hazards confined to the workplace setting. They categorised COVID as "day-to-day dangers that all face," just like crime and air pollution.

It is noteworthy that several earlier case laws in the United States supported vaccine mandates. The most notable among them is *Jacobson v. Massachusetts* (1905)[2]. In this case, the U.S. Supreme Court upheld a Massachusetts law that required individuals to be vaccinated against smallpox. The Court ruled that the state had the power to enact such a law in the interest of public health and that the individual's right to refuse vaccination was not absolute. The learned judges had, in another ruling observed that "Jacobson hardly supports cutting the Constitution loose during a pandemic[3]." The Jacobson ruling did not contravene the Constitution of the United States or infringe on any right granted or secured by the Constitution. The recent COVID-19 mandates denied many services and suspended rights if the person did not get vaccinated, thereby violating the constitutional and fundamental rights of the people.

The United States Supreme Court, in essence, reiterated the stance that vaccine mandates will be legal and ethical as long as they are implemented in a fair and non-discriminatory manner and are based on evidence-based recommendations. Also, vaccine mandates cannot be sweeping, and exceptions need to be made for individuals with certain medical conditions or disabilities that make vaccination contraindicated, or for individuals who have sincerely held religious or philosophical beliefs that conflict with vaccination.

[1]*The National Federation of Business vs the Department of Labor* , 595 U. S. ____ (2022)

[2]*Jacobson v. Massachusetts, 197 U.S. 11 (1905)*

[3] Roman Catholic Diocese of Brooklyn, New York v Andrew M Cuomo, Governor of New York(2020), 592 U. S. ____ (2020)

CHAPTER TEN

The latest Supreme Court verdict in India

In *Jacob Puliyel vs Union of India*[1] on **2 May 2022, the** Supreme Court of India delivered a similar, if not stronger, judgment against vaccine mandates, compared to *the National Federation of Business vs the Department of Labor.* **The Court held that the state or any authority cannot force** an individual to get vaccinated against COVID-19, and the right to bodily integrity of a person under Article 21 of the Constitution includes the right to refuse vaccination. The Court also held that the vaccine mandates imposed by various state governments and other authorities in the context of the COVID-19 pandemic, which tend to deny access to basic welfare measures and freedom of movement to unvaccinated individuals, are "not proportionate".

These recent verdicts affirm the sacrosanct nature of fundamental rights, especially the right to bodily autonomy. The fundamental rights guaranteed by the Constitution is not "fair-weather" right that any authority can suspend at will during a crisis.

[1] Jacob Puliyel vs Union of India *(2022)* W.P. (Civil) No. 607 of 2021

www.ingramcontent.com/pod-product-compliance
Lightning Source LLC
Chambersburg PA
CBHW071259140726
47996CB00007B/2912